GRADE **6** SIX

POWERTHINK
Cooperative Critical Thinking Activities

Written by Cindy Barden

Illustrated by Gary Mohrmann

D1508845

Editor: Hanna Otero

Cover Design: Kristin Lock

Graphic Artists: Danielle Dela Cruz and Anthony Strasburger

Note on reproduction of this material: No part of this publication may be reproduced, stored in a retrieval system, or transmitted, in any form or by any means—electronic, mechanical, recording, or otherwise—without prior permission of the publisher. Reproduction of workbook activity pages by classroom teacher for use in the classroom and not for commercial sale is permissible. Reproduction of these materials for an entire school system is strictly forbidden.

FSI12115 POWERTHINK–Grade Six
All rights reserved-Printed in the U.S.A.
Copyright ©2000 Frank Schaffer Publications
23740 Hawthorne Blvd., Torrance, CA 90505

Table of Contents

Introduction...4

POWERTHINKING 5

What Makes a Good Thinker?.....................6

Non-Content Activities.....................7-18

    Can It? 7

    Headline History 8

    How High is Up? 9

    How is an Elephant Like a Mouse? 10

    Apple or Cherry?.....................11

    Is It a Bird? 12

    I Can Hear What You're Painting 13

    Take Two Aspirins and Call Me in the Morning..14

    Famous or Notorious? 15

    Chirp, Chirp, Boom, Creak.....................16

    Riddle Me 17

    Classification Puzzle 18

Language Arts Activities 19-26

    Dr. Livingstone, I Presume 19

    Step by Step 20

    Three-part Story 21

    From A to Z 22

    First, the Beginning 23

    And Now, the Ending.....................24

    And the Winner Is 25

    Distress Signals 26

Social Studies Activities 27-35

    Flashing, Crackling, Booming.....................27

    That Might Work! 28

    Both Sides Are Important 29

    Ad Savvy 30

    Advertising Report Card.....................31

    Why Do We Have Holidays? 32

    Can You Be More Specific?.....................33

    Whom Would You Hire? 34

    Show, Don't Tell 35

Mathematics Activities.....................36-40

    Are Sales Up or Down? 36

    Alligator Repellent.....................37

    Not a Rectangle 38

    Not a Math Test 39

    Magic Square 40

Science Activities 41-46

    Invent It! 41

    Reduce, Reuse, Recycle 42

    Lima Beans Are Green 43

    Peregrine Falcons Are Endangered 44

    You're the Inventor.....................45

    Mercury Olympics 46

Art Activities 47-52

    A Terrific Toy 47

    Show Me 48

    Your Family Flag 49

    Do You Follow Me?.....................50

    Did You Follow That? 51

    Make a Mobile Point 52

Problem Solving Activities 53-61

    Decisions, Decisions, Decisions.....................53

    What Are Your Options?.....................54

    Getting Closer 55

    Finally.....................56

    What, Me Worry?.....................57

    Getting a Handle on Worries 58

    Seeing the Other Side 59

    Maybe There's Another Way 60

    Using the Tools.....................61

Encouraging POWERTHINKING 62

Bibliography.....................63

Answers 64

INTRODUCTION

"There are one-story intellects, two-story intellects and three-story intellects with skylights. All fact collectors who have no aim beyond their facts are one-story people. Two-story people compare, reason, generalize, using the labor of the fact collectors as their own. Three-story people idealize, imagine, predict – their best illumination comes from above through the skylight."

Oliver Wendell Holmes

As educators, our goal is to assist students to become "third-story thinkers." Both the National Council of Teachers of Mathematics and the National Science Teachers Association recommend including problem solving and decision making as major goals of education.

What is critical thinking? Research indicates that the skill most basic to critical thinking is the ability to listen or read actively while continuously analyzing the information being presented. Sounds pretty basic, doesn't it? This ability requires the learner to be able to engage in an internal dialogue. Effective learners can dialogue internally without skipping steps.

Current recommendations suggest that children can best learn critical thinking skills by working in small groups or pairs. Working in pairs forces students to externalize their thinking – to think aloud, and to identify errors and skipped steps. It also teaches students to recognize and edit unsystematic thinking in themselves and others.

The **POWERTHINK** series of reproducible activity sheets is designed to provide cooperative learning opportunities for either small groups or pairs. There are six levels of challenge in the **POWERTHINK** series, allowing you to introduce critical thinking material at a sequential pace.

POWERTHINK has provided you with activity sheets that pertain to the major content areas of language arts, social studies, mathematics, science, art, and problem solving.

The **POWERTHINK** activity books have been designed to provide practice in:

Evaluating Information
Differentiating Between Fact and Opinion
Looking at Both Sides of an Issue
Solving Problems
Making Decisions
Observation
Synthesis
Searching for Alternative Solutions
Exploring New Ideas
Identifying and Clarifying
Setting Goals
Deductive Reasoning
Pre-planning
Giving and Following Directions
Comparing and Contrasting
Brainstorming
Predicting
Organizing Material

Because the teaching of critical thinking skills can also be a forum for truly individual positive reinforcement, on page 63 you will find a list of powerful verbal reinforcers. Use these to encourage your students as they become "**POWERTHINKERS.**"

Happy **POWERTHINKING!**

What is **THINKING?**

Thinking can be many things. To see that this is true, try this:

DON'T THINK! Close your eyes for one minute and do not think of anything at all.

Did it work? Did you find yourself thinking about something? Or thinking about how you weren't supposed to be thinking?

So, where and when do you think? In school, of course. That's obvious. But if you're thinking all the time, there must be other times and places for thinking. You are also thinking when you…

- read a magazine
- decide which television program to watch
- climb a tree
- go for a walk in the country
- write a letter
- play a video game
- go on a vacation with your family
- listen to your grandparents tell about "the old days"
- lie on your back and look at the clouds
- get into an argument

Remember: there are many ways to think. And you're thinking all the time.

Now, what is **POWERTHINKING?**

POWERTHINKING is powerful thinking.

The power of thinking is greater than all other kinds of power combined! Think about the person who discovered that a wheel made it a lot easier to move a big rock. That person's brainpower was stronger than a whole team of big, muscular rock movers. You can use **POWERTHINKING** to solve problems that are too big for any other type of power!

Can you remember a time when you used thinking to solve a problem, make a really tough decision, or get out of a jam? Thinking gives you POWER. Power to turn a bad situation into a good one, to turn a defeat into a victory, and even to make someone with hurt feelings feel better. There is no limit to your thinking power. And, there are lots of ways to make your thinking even more powerful than it already is!

Every page in your **POWERTHINK** book will have a little area called "**LIGHTNING STRIKES.**" This is the place for you to write down whatever flashes into your mind as you're doing the activity on the page. Like real lightning strikes, these stray thoughts come and go in a split second. So when you have a lightning strike, write it down quickly, before you forget it. Some of these strikes are going to be pretty wacky. But write them all down anyway. You can always cross out the sillier lightning strikes later, or transfer them to a silly thoughts file. But maybe, just maybe, that nutty idea will lead you to think about a problem in a new way. The lightning strike may not be the answer you want, but it may lead you to the answer you are looking for. So remember: write down whatever is on your mind. Try it! You'll be amazed at the powerful stuff that flashes around in your brain.

Each activity in your **POWERTHINK** book also includes a "**POWER PLAY.**" POWER PLAYS are questions that will challenge you and take you and your powerful thinking machine one step further.

POWERTHINKING asks you to look at your mind as a muscle. The more you use it, the stronger it gets. If you keep using it, keep stretching it, before long, you'll be thinking with real power. That's what **POWERTHINKING** is all about: learning to use and strengthen your mind. You will find that you can use **POWERTHINKING** at school, but you will also use it at home, during vacations, and for the rest of your life!

WHAT MAKES A GOOD THINKER?

Are some people better thinkers than others?

Someone could be a great hockey player and not so good at tennis. A person can be well-educated and know a lot about a subject, but he or she may not necessarily be a great thinker.

Thinking is a skill that can be learned. If you wanted to kick field goals, you would practice every day. If you wanted to be an Olympic gymnast, you would spend many, many hours practicing. So how do you learn to be a better thinker?

Work with a partner. List some qualities that make a person a good thinker.

Thinkers You Know

List some people who are good at thinking. Include friends, people you know, or people you have read about.

Here is an example: <u>Jason</u> is a good thinker because <u>he often thinks of new ways to solve problems.</u>

POWER PLAY
It takes practice....practice....practice....to get better at a task, whether it's soccer, playing the piano...or thinking.

_____is a good thinker because _____

_____

_____is a good thinker because _____

_____

_____is a good thinker because _____

_____

CAN IT?

"If you make people think they are thinking, they will love you. If you make them really think, they will hate you."
—Author Unknown

Why do people hate to think? Could it be mental laziness? What are some other reasons?

Here's a warm-up exercise to get your brain thinking.
A **POWERTHINKER** looks at ordinary objects in new ways, asks questions, and comes up with new ideas.

How many uses can you and your partner think of for an empty soup can? Write them below.

_____

_____

_____

What if the can were 100 times smaller? How would that change its possible uses? Now what would it be good for?

_____

_____

_____

What could the can be used for if it were 100 times larger than normal?

_____

_____

_____

POWER PLAY
What other objects could have uses other than the usual ones? Challenge a friend to think of ten uses for a block of wood, a marble, and a piece of string.

HEADLINE HISTORY

A headline quickly summarizes a story or an article in a newspaper or magazine. Its purpose is to get people interested enough to read the article. Headlines are short and to the point.

Write five headlines about events that have happened in your life. You could include special events like winning a contest or an award, getting a good report card, moving to a new city, or passing a difficult test. You could use ordinary events like getting up in the morning, eating meatloaf for supper, or oversleeping on a school day.

For this activity, the events aren't the important part. Make the headlines short and interesting.

POWER PLAY

By using the right words as a beginning, you can get people interested in learning the rest of the story. Before you can communicate with someone, you need to get their attention.

Design a magazine devoted entirely to you and your life. Give the magazine a name. Decide on what departments or sections your magazine will have. Design a cover and write a typical story for the magazine.

The Tuesday   Morning Edition

Hollerin' Herald

_____

_____

_____

_____

_____

LIGHTNING STRIKES

HOW HIGH IS UP?

A good way to practice **POWERTHINKING** is by asking questions, even if you don't always get answers. Sometimes, what's most important is thinking about the questions.

Is pink shorter than red?
How do zippers work?
What if clocks ran backwards half the time?
What does blue sound like?
What if everyone in the world had the same name?
Why doesn't yellow smell like green?

Try your hand at writing some "what ifs." Work with a partner and write five questions like the ones above — make them silly, weird, unusual, or different. You don't have to know the answers. There doesn't even have to be an answer.

1. _____
2. _____
3. _____
4. _____
5. _____

Select one of your questions. Write down as many thoughts and ideas about the topic that you and your partner can think of. Be as outrageous as you want.

POWER PLAY

How can asking questions help you think better? Have you asked any good questions today?

Make a list of five commonly-heard questions that would sound outrageous or weird to people of 200 years ago. For example: "How long did it take you to fly from New York to Los Angeles?"

Are there any questions that you came up with in this activity that might not seem so silly 200 years from now?

HOW IS AN ELEPHANT LIKE A MOUSE?

Elephants and mice are not at all alike. Or are they?

Both are mammals. Both have tails. Both have four legs. Both eat grains. Both drink water. What other ways are they alike?

To compare means to look at ways that items or ideas are alike.

Work with a partner. Randomly select two numbers from 1 to 9. Write the numbers here: _____ and _____.

Use your numbers to take one item from column A and one from column B. For example, if your numbers are 1 and 3, your two items would be Owl and Brick wall.

Column A	Column B
1. Owl	1. Student
2. Shoe	2. Blanket
3. Person	3. Brick wall
4. Table	4. Ceiling
5. Toe	5. Hammer
6. Roller skates	6. Shirt
7. Octopus	7. Paint brush
8. Library	8. Penguin
9. Flute	9. Sandpaper

POWER PLAY

Comparing two unlike items or ideas can help you see ways they are alike.

Our two items are _____ and _____.

Talk about ways these two things are alike. List at least 10 similarities.

APPLE OR CHERRY?

How is a poem different from a story? How is an apple pie different from a cherry pie?

Contrasting means looking at ways objects or ideas are different.

Work with a partner to contrast each set of words. List several ways they are different.

How is a WEEKEND different from a VACATION?

_____

_____

_____

How does a CLOCK differ from a WATCH?

_____

_____

_____

How are FLOWERS and TREES different?

_____

_____

_____

POWER PLAY

Sometimes ideas, products, people, or objects seem much the same at first. How can looking at ways they are different help you make decisions?

IS IT A BIRD?

A claim is a statement that might be true or false. As a **POWERTHINKER**, you will always be on the lookout for claims that might not be true. Sometimes you can do this by observation. You can use your senses of sight, hearing, smell, taste and touch.

You and your friend see an object far up in the sky. You say it is a bird. He says it's a plane. Which sense besides sight could you use to find out?

You could listen. If you hear a motor, it's probably not a bird. If it quacks, it's probably not an airplane.

If your mother says the chicken soup is too salty, you could taste it and find out for yourself.

Work with a partner. Talk about different situations where your senses could help you decide if something is true or false.

List some ways you use your sense of touch at home.

_____

_____

_____

List some ways you use your senses of sight and hearing in sports.

_____

_____

_____

List some ways you use your senses of smell and taste in a restaurant.

_____

_____

_____

POWER PLAY
Your senses tell you much about what is going on around you and help you make decisions about the truth of claims.

LIGHTNING STRIKES

Is it a bird?

Is it a plane?

It's... POWERTHINKER!

I CAN HEAR WHAT YOU'RE PAINTING

With a partner, design one or more of the following items. Draw a picture and write a few sentences about how your invention works.

1. A telephone with a "ring" that can also be observed with the sense of smell.

2. A book that can also be read with the sense of taste.

3. A computer game in which players can rely only on the sense of touch.

4. A stereo that plays music that can also be "experienced" with the sense of sight.

5. Paint that has a different sound for every color, for use in paintings that can be heard as well as seen.

POWER PLAY
With a partner think what really cool thing you wish you had that hasn't been invented yet. Draw a picture of your invention.

Frank Schaffer Publications

TAKE TWO ASPIRINS AND CALL ME IN THE MORNING

It is reasonable to accept a claim if it comes from a reliable source and does not conflict with what you have observed for yourself, what you have learned by experience, or what other credible sources claim.

An **expert** is someone who has learned much about a subject through training, education, and experience. Even if a person is an expert in one area, that person may not be a reliable source in other areas.

If your doctor tells you your car needs new brakes, would that be a reliable source? Probably not, unless the doctor also happened to be a mechanic.

Would you consider these sources reliable? Why or why not?

Your neighbor tells you he can solve the budget deficit in three simple steps. _____

_____

A nurse suggests you should rest and drink plenty of fluids when you have a cold. _____

_____

A famous scientist says he has found a way to reverse gravity.

_____

_____

A famous tennis player on a television commercial tells you to buy Iceberg Cereal._____

_____

A famous novelist writes an article about how to learn to ice skate.

_____

_____

A fire fighter talks to your class about ways to prevent fires.

_____

_____

POWER PLAY

Why is it important for a POWERTHINKER to know if a source is reliable? How can you find out if a source is reliable?

With a partner, go through a newspaper or magazine article, looking for sources who are mentioned or quoted. Classify each source as Probably Reliable, Probably Not Reliable, or Can't Tell. Give reasons for your classifications.

FAMOUS OR NOTORIOUS?

To understand claims you read or hear, it is important to understand all the words. If you don't know the meaning of a word, you can look it up in a dictionary or other source.

However, the true meaning of a word often goes beyond its dictionary definition. These extra meanings are called **connotations**. Two words can have almost the same definition, but mean different things because they have positive or negative connotations.

Would you rather be notorious or famous? Even though both words are defined as well-known, most people think of someone crooked when they hear the word notorious and someone special or admired when they hear the word famous. Notorious has a negative connotation, while famous has a positive connotation.

Work with a partner. Look at each word. Talk about whether the word has a negative or positive connotation. Write a **P** after the word if you think it has a positive connotation and an **N** if you think it's negative. Be prepared to explain your answers.

POWER PLAY

Why is it important to understand not only the dictionary definition of a word, but also the connotation? How are words used to influence people?

With a partner, look through the real estate section of the classified ads in your local newspaper. Make a list of words used to describe the homes in the ads. For each positive word try to think of a negative term that might be more realistic. For example, "cozy" is a positive term for a small house, while "cramped" or "crackerbox" are negative.

Determined	_____	Stubborn	_____
Thrifty	_____	Stingy	_____
Skinny	_____	Thin	_____
Petite	_____	Short	_____
Fragrance	_____	Odor	_____
Average	_____	Mediocre	_____
Outspoken	_____	Assertive	_____
Unusual	_____	Peculiar	_____
Innocent	_____	Naive	_____

Frank Schaffer Publications

CHIRP, CHIRP, BOOM, CREAK

You're home alone and hear sounds coming from the basement. The noises sound like CHIRP, CHIRP, BOOM, CREAK. You could go downstairs and look, but you really don't want to do that.

What could be making those noises? Work with a partner to think of as many possible noisemakers as you can. List them below.

_____

_____

_____

_____

_____

_____

When you run out of ideas, ask your teacher for a hint that may help you come up with more ideas.

_____

_____

_____

_____

_____

_____

POWER PLAY

Did the hint help you come up with additional ideas? There's not always one right answer.

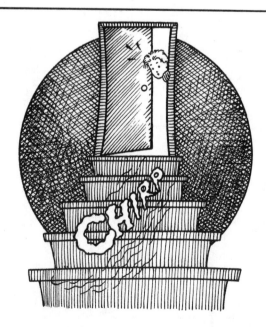

RIDDLE ME

Why did the chicken cross the road?

Because he wanted to go to the mall.
Because he left his hat there.
Because the duck was waiting for him on the other side.

A **POWERTHINKER** learns to look at familiar objects, problems, and ideas in new ways, to come up with new solutions and new ideas.

Work with a partner to think up five reasons why the alligator crossed the road.

Because _____

_____

Because _____

_____

Because _____

_____

Because _____

_____

Because _____

_____

How about another one? How many answers can you and your partner come up with for this riddle: What do you get when you cross a skunk with a baseball?

_____

_____

_____

_____

POWER PLAY

Questions may have more than one right answer. The first answer you think of may not be the best one or the only one. Keep looking, and you may be surprised at the good or imaginative answers you come up with!

FS112115 POWERTHINK

Frank Schaffer Publications

CLASSIFICATION PUZZLE

A big part of **POWERTHINKING** is being able to classify and categorize things, whether those things are ideas, arguments, people, pros and cons, or possible alternatives. Here's a little practice in categorizing, using the letters of the alphabet.

1. The letters of the alphabet have been divided into two groups. Identify them.

GROUP 1: _____ GROUP 2: _____

    A E I O U   B C D F G H J K L M N P Q R S T V W X Y Z

2. Too easy? Try this: Again, the letters of the alphabet have been divided into two groups. Identify them.

GROUP 1: _____ GROUP 2: _____

    A E F H I K L M N T V W X Y Z   B C D G J O P Q R S U

3. Getting the hang of it? Now try this one:

GROUP 1: _____ GROUP 2: _____

    A B E F G H J K N O P Q R S T U W Y Z   C D I L M V X

POWER PLAY

Now, you try to make up a classification puzzle! Divide the letters of the alphabet — or anything else, for that matter— into two groups and have a partner try to guess your classification scheme. Then let your partner try to stump you with a classification puzzle.

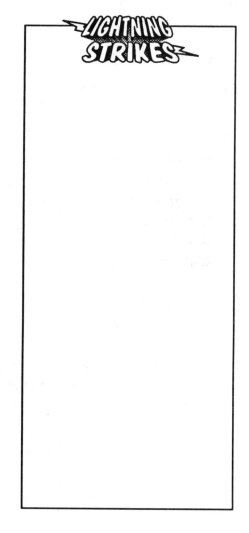

DR. LIVINGSTONE, I PRESUME

Authors don't always give every detail of an action or event.
Sometimes you can "read between the lines" and make inferences. This means that you interpret what is meant, make guesses about what happened, or draw conclusions from evidence presented.

Read the following paragraph.

Shelly trudged wearily up the steep hill pushing her bicycle.
"Why does everything go wrong in weather like this?" she sighed
to herself, wiping the sweat from her forehead and leaving streaks
of grease from her hands. "Now I'll probably be late again."

Read the statements below and talk about them with a partner. Decide if the statements are probably true using the information in the above paragraph. Put a check mark in front of the correct inferences.

1. (   )   Shelly is coming home from school.

2. (   )   Shelly lives at the top of a hill.

3. (   )   It is a warm day.

4. (   )   Shelly has been late before.

5. (   )   Shelly's bicycle is broken and she tried to fix it.

6. (   )   Shelly is going to her piano lesson.

Now read the next paragraph. On the back of this sheet, list some inferences that can be made from the information given.

The last rays of the setting sun glittered off the shiny metal of Ted's weight-lifting equipment. Even with the garage door open, the breeze wasn't enough to keep him cool. He wiped the sweat from his face and neck with a towel and threw a second one to Bart. "Not a bad workout this time," Ted told his friend. "Let's get together tomorrow, same time, same place."

POWER PLAY

Write a short story about something that happened to you recently. Exchange papers with your partner. List some inferences that can be made from what your partner wrote.

STEP BY STEP

Have you ever read directions that were so confusing that even Albert Einstein would have had trouble?

To describe how to do a task, you need to break down the task into steps and list them in order.

Think about the steps needed for a simple task like tying your shoes or drawing a circle. What equipment do you need? What do you do first? Then what?

To draw a circle, the first step might be: Decide how large the circle should be and where you want to draw it.

Think about the steps needed to complete these tasks:

Nail two pieces of wood together.

Sew a button on a shirt.

Look up a word in a dictionary.

Play a movie on a VCR.

Make a hard-boiled egg.

Put a new battery in a radio.

Cut out a paper snowflake.

Call someone whose telephone number you don't know.

Hang a picture on the wall.

Make a peanut butter and jelly sandwich.

Select one of the tasks. Talk about the steps needed with your partner before you start writing. Use the back of this page to list every step needed to complete the task. Don't skip any steps, even if they seem obvious. Don't forget to include the equipment needed and how to use it. If you forget a step, add it at the end and use an arrow to show where it goes.

_____

_____

_____

_____

_____

POWER PLAY

You need to be able to think clearly before you can write clearly. How can breaking a task into steps help you think and write clearly?

Pick another task from the list or make up your own. Write a set of directions for the task, but leave out one or two important steps. Give the directions to a partner to see if he or she can identify the missing steps.

THREE-PART STORY

Stories have a beginning, a middle, and an ending.

The Beginning:

The beginning of a story usually sets the scene by describing the main characters and the situation.

Take a clean sheet of paper and write the beginning of a story. Or use the back of this sheet. You can stop at a point where something exciting is about to happen.

Take your time and use your best handwriting because other people will need to be able to read it. Write on lined paper. If you're stuck for a beginning, you could use one of these ideas:

> An alligator makes a wish.
>
> Josh moves to a new city.
>
> Sara hits a home run in a big game.
>
> A kangaroo finds something unusual in her pocket.
>
> Paula travels to the other side of the rainbow.
>
> Simon overhears a conversation between two trees.

The Middle:

The middle of a story gives additional information about the characters and carries on the story line. Trade papers with a classmate. Read what the first person wrote. Now write a middle for that story, using the characters and situation that the first person started with. Don't write the ending.

The Ending:

The ending "wraps up" the story by solving the problem or giving some type of conclusion.

Trade papers with another classmate. (Be sure you don't get your own beginning.) Read what the first two people wrote. Now, using that story, write an ending.

When everyone has finished, give the story back to the person who started it. Take turns reading your stories out loud from beginning to end. Were you surprised at what happened and how it ended? Did it end the way you thought it would?

POWER PLAY

With a partner, write a story about a weekend you'd like to have together. What would you do? Where would you go? How would the weekend end?

Don't forget the beginning, the middle, and the ending.

Name(s)_____

FROM A TO Z

Mix the right ingredients, in the right order, and you'll have a delicious, light, fluffy chocolate cake. Mix the right words, in the right order, and you can get an exciting story or essay. Unfortunately, there's no recipe for an interesting story like there is for a chocolate cake.

One way to make your writing more interesting is to use descriptive words. Which sentence tells you more?

The man drove his car fast.

The 60 year old man drove his red Mustang convertible 80 miles an hour.

Write a more descriptive version of this sentence:

The woman sat on the grass.

_____

_____

When you write about a subject, think of many descriptive words before you start. To help you do this, make an ABC checklist.

Finish this sentence by writing at least one word that begins with each letter of the alphabet. Skip around if you like. Write more than one word for each letter if you can.

The sea was agitated, _____, _____...

A. agitated

B. _____

C. _____

D. _____

E. _____

F. _____

G. _____

H. _____

I. _____

J. jade-green

K. _____

L. _____

M. _____

N. _____

O. _____

P. _____

Q. _____

R. _____

S. stormy

T. _____

U. _____

V. _____

W. _____

X. _____

Y. _____

Z. _____

POWER PLAY

Making a list of descriptive words about a subject or character first can help you write a story or essay.

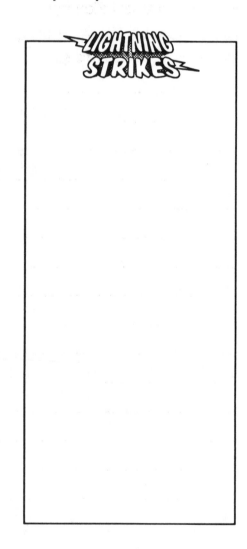

FIRST, THE BEGINNING

Have you ever turned on the television in the middle of a movie and wondered what had happened before you started watching? Have you ever missed the ending to an interesting show? That can be annoying. Here's your chance to write the beginning and the ending of a story.

First, read the middle:

> Carlos felt his way along the dark, windowless hallway searching for a light switch. He wished he still had his dad's flashlight. With his right hand touching the side of the cold, clammy stone wall and his left hand in front of him to brush away the sticky cobwebs, he moved forward slowly. Without warning Carlos bumped into a solid wooden door. As he reached for the doorknob, he heard some very unusual sounds coming from behind the door. He wondered if he should turn around and try to find his way back or take a chance with what was behind the door.

What happened in the beginning? Why was Carlos alone in a dark hallway? What was he looking for? What happened to his flashlight?

Work with a partner to write the beginning of the story. Talk about your ideas before you start writing.

_____

_____

_____

_____

_____

_____

_____

_____

_____

_____

_____

_____

_____

Continue with this activity on the next page.

AND NOW, THE ENDING

Read your beginning and the middle of the story about Carlos.

What happened in the end? Did Carlos try to go back? Did he open the door? What did he find?

Write the ending to this story.

_____
_____
_____
_____
_____
_____
_____
_____
_____
_____

POWER PLAY

The ending an author writes for a story may not be the best one possible. There could be many endings.

With a partner, list at least five movies you have both seen. For each movie, write a new ending. Read your ideas to others in your class. What do they think of your new ending?

What's the title of your story?_____

Share your story with others. Read the different versions written by your classmates. There are no wrong beginnings and endings to this story, but you may like some better than others.

FS112115 POWERTHINK

Name(s)_____

AND THE WINNER IS...

Awards are given for best actor, best script, best rap song, best country/western song, etc. Today's contest is for best fictional character in a short story or novel.

Here are some possible categories:

Funniest	Tallest	Best animal
Scariest	Shortest	Most talkative
Most serious	Youngest	Bravest
Most unique	Oldest	

Enter your favorite fictional character in one of these categories or make up your own category.

Category: _____

Character's name: _____

List some words and phrases to describe your character.

_____   _____

_____   _____

_____   _____

Use these words and phrases to write a paragraph about why your character is the best in a category. In 100 words or less, why does this character deserve to win?

_____

_____

_____

_____

_____

_____

_____

_____

_____

_____

_____

_____

POWER PLAY

With your partner, discuss what the awards ceremony might be like. Talk about what the awards might be. Draw a picture of your character receiving his or her award.

Name(s)_____

DISTRESS SIGNALS

Joanie is piloting a small research plane over the snow-covered Rocky Mountains when engine trouble forces her to land. She works on the engine for over four hours before finally giving up. She's stranded in the mountains in winter and has only a gallon of water and enough food for one meal. Plus, the plane has come to rest underneath some trees, making it impossible to see from the air. Yet, she's not worried. Joanie gets right to work gathering pine boughs and carefully laying them out on an open field of snow. Within a few hours, she is spotted by a plane passing overhead, and a rescue party follows the next day.

This is what Joanie made in
the snow with the pine boughs:

The symbol means *aircraft damaged,*
and it is recognized by pilots around the
world. In fact, pilots have made up a complete set of simple distress symbols that can be constructed so that they are visible from the air.

1. With a partner, do some **POWERTHINKING** and see how many you can identify:

a.   b.   c.

d.   e. F   f. N

2. Now list some ways that you could construct symbols like these in each of the following crash sites. Think about the materials you would have at hand in each environment.

   a. forest

   b. desert

   c. grassland

POWER PLAY
With a partner, make up new symbols and messages to add to the assortment of distress signals pictured at left.

FLASHING, CRACKLING, BOOMING

What is **brainstorming**? Is it thunder and lightning in your head? Not exactly, but sometimes ideas do seem to flash and crash in your brain.

Brainstorming is a **POWERTHINKER'S** way of working with others to come up with ideas to solve problems. Each member of the group says his or her thoughts out loud and someone writes them down. It doesn't matter if the ideas are good or bad, practical or completely off the wall. The purpose is to get as many ideas as possible. You can talk about the ideas later.

Select one of the topics listed below and start brainstorming. One person can write the ideas on the back of this sheet. Don't worry about complete sentences. Avoid negative comments like "That's a dumb idea," or "That would never work."

1. Can wars be prevented? How?

2. What are some ways kids our age can earn money?

3. What does it mean to be a good neighbor?

4. What responsibilities do voters have?

5. How could taxes be reduced?

6. How could a busy intersection be made safe?

7. How could pollution from car exhaust be reduced?

POWER PLAY

Talk about these questions with a partner: How could brainstorming with family members help you plan a vacation or solve a problem at home? How could brainstorming with friends help you decide what to do on a rainy Saturday? How could brainstorming with classmates help you understand a book you've read?

Frank Schaffer Publications

Name(s)_____

THAT MIGHT WORK!

When you brainstorm, you quickly write down all ideas, without deciding if they are "good" or "bad." Once you've done some heavy-duty brainstorming, what do you do with all those ideas? Now it's time to evaluate them — to look at each one and decide which ones could actually work.

Suppose someone suggested getting rid of all weapons as a way of ending war. It would be a great idea, but how would you do it?

Ask each person in the group to select two or three of the ideas from "Flashing, Crackling, and Booming." Write them on this page. As a group, consider each one individually. Think out loud, talk about an idea, discuss how or why it would or wouldn't work. Write one sentence after each idea that explains why your group thought it would or wouldn't work.

POWER PLAY

An idea might be very good, but it might not work for many reasons. An idea might seem silly or strange at first but, after thinking about it, you may find it's just right. When you evaluate an idea, spend plenty of time thinking about it.

The topic our group discussed was: _____

Idea: _____

Reason:_____

Idea: _____

Reason:_____

Idea: _____

Reason:_____

Idea: _____

Reason:_____

Idea: _____

Reason:_____

Idea: _____

Reason:_____

Idea: _____

Reason:_____

Use the back of this page if you need more room to write.

That might work!

BOTH SIDES ARE IMPORTANT

What if someone suggested that all students wear uniforms to school every day? The uniform would be navy blue skirts or pants (no jeans) and a white blouse or shirt. (Girls could wear skirts or pants.) A navy blue sweater or jacket would be acceptable, but t-shirts, sweatshirts, and other colors would not.

Hold your opinion for now and spend some time thinking about both sides of the issue. Work with a partner to come up with ideas for and against uniforms. Try to see each side of the issue objectively. List your ideas.

Why school students should wear uniforms	Why school students should not wear uniforms

POWER PLAY

Looking at both sides of an issue can help you see other points of view. You might even change your mind. Even if you don't change your mind, you may understand someone better after you hear what they have to say. LISTENING and looking at both sides of an issue are POWERTHINKING skills too.

AD SAVVY

Most ads (except those on radio) blend pictures and words into a message: Buy this product. Vote for this candidate. Give up a bad habit. Change your mind. Go here on vacation. Join the Army.

The message can be communicated in many different ways. Here are a few popular techniques:

COMPARISON: Our product is better than the others: "The Datatel has more memory and better graphics than any other computer on the market."

BANDWAGON: Everyone is doing it, and you should, too: "Taste tests show that 83 percent of grape juice drinkers drink O.K. Fine juice."

FLATTERY: You're a great person, so you need this great product: "Only smart, good-looking, successful walkers wear Durasoles."

EXPERTS: "Four out of five barbers recommend HairKare combs."

Some ads simply list reasons for buying a product or voting for a candidate. Some use music or scenery to make people feel good when they think of a product. Some use humor. And sometimes, a celebrity will endorse a product or service in an advertisement.

With a little practice in **POWERTHINKING,** you can learn to be critical about the advertising you see every day. Make copies of the Advertising Report Card printed on the next page. With a partner, look through newspapers and magazines for advertisements. When you see an ad that looks interesting, cut it out. Then fill out and attach a Report Card. Keep a notebook of ads that you've reported on, or post the ads on a bulletin board. You can also use the report card to report on television and radio advertising.

POWER PLAY

As a group, keep a log of television advertisements during one Saturday. Try early morning, mid-afternoon, and early evening. What type of advertisements do you see the most of during the morning? The afternoon? The evening? What audiences are these advertisements aimed at? Why do you think advertisers use these time slots as they do?

Discuss your findings with your group and compare your answers.

Name(s)_____

ADVERTISING REPORT CARD

Your Name for the Ad:_____

Product or Service:_____

Type of Ad: _____

    Newspaper   Magazine   Television

    Radio   Mail   Other_____

Advertising Technique:

    Bandwagon   Experts   Celebrities

    Fear   Happiness   Comparison

    Flattery   Humor   Other_____

Images used (including photographs, drawings, video, animation, charts, and so forth): _____

_____

_____

Key phrases or words: _____

_____

The most important part of this advertisement:_____

_____

Is there any misleading information in the ad?

_____

_____

Does this ad make you want to buy the product or service being advertised? Why or why not?

_____

_____

_____

_____

POWER PLAY

With a partner, make up an advertisement to convince other students that your school is the school they should attend.

WHY DO WE HAVE HOLIDAYS?

Think of some holidays we celebrate. What makes a day so important that everyone gets a day off from school or work? Work with a partner to make a list of reasons that we have holidays. Talk about your ideas, then write them below.

_____

_____

_____

_____

_____

If you could make up a holiday, what would you celebrate? Someone's birthday? A day in honor of your favorite food? A day in honor of an animal, a place, a planet, an idea?

Work with your partner to think of a new holiday.

The name of the new holiday would be_____

_____

The reason for celebrating this holiday would be_____

_____

On what date would the holiday be celebrated? _____

_____

Typical foods eaten on this holiday: _____

_____

Songs and games connected with the holiday: _____

_____

Fictional characters or special animals: _____

_____

Colors especially associated with the holiday: _____

_____

POWER PLAY

Work with your partner to list ways people could celebrate your holiday.

Happy Aardvark Day

CAN YOU BE MORE SPECIFIC?

Statements which do not contain clear, specific information are **vague**. "Teresa is tall" is a vague statement. "Teresa is six feet, three inches tall" is a specific statement.

Words like big, tall, short, small, fast, slow, many, some, and several are examples of vague words. How big? How tall? How short? How small? How fast? How slow? How many?

When you read or listen to someone speak, be aware of vague statements. Question vague claims.

Many health professionals recommend Iceberg Cereal.

Many? Does that mean 12? 42? 4,691? 93%?

What is meant by health professionals? Doctors? X-ray technicians? Dentists?

Read this report about Chicago, then circle the vague words and phrases.

Chicago is a big city. Lots of people live there. In fact, it's one of the biggest in the United States. Sometimes Chicago is called the Windy City because it's windy there. A long time ago a big fire destroyed much of the city and left many people without a place to live, but people rebuilt and now a lot of really tall buildings can be found in Chicago. There are many attractions for visitors to see and a very busy airport there. I think I'd like to visit Chicago someday.

Now look at this second report about Chicago. Find the specific facts and circle them.

With a population of 2,783,726, Chicago is the largest city in Illinois and the third largest in the United States. Situated on the southwestern shore of Lake Michigan, Chicago has been nicknamed the Windy City because of the high winds that frequently blow off the lake.

The city's impressive skyline includes one of the world's tallest buildings, the 1,454-foot Sears Tower. Chicago's O'Hare Airport is the busiest in the U.S. In 1871 a fire left nearly 100,000 people homeless. The Museum of Science and Industry is one of many tourist attractions in Chicago.

POWER PLAY

*A **POWERTHINKER** questions vague statements and looks for specifics. Look for specifics when you read. Include specifics when you write.*

Name(s)_____

WHOM WOULD YOU HIRE?

If you apply for a job, someone in charge will probably ask you questions to see if you are right for the job. To ask the right questions, he or she needs to know what skills or knowledge are needed for the job.

Help Wanted...

Someone to teach sixth-grade science.
Someone to coach a Little League baseball team.
Someone to baby-sit for a one-year-old child.
Someone to paint the top floor of a 23-story building.
Someone to care for your alligator while you are on vacation.

Select one of the jobs above. Work with a partner. List types of skills and knowledge a person would need to do that job well.

If I hired someone to _____

that person should know_____

_____

that person should be able to_____

_____

that person should be interested in_____

_____

that person should enjoy_____

_____

POWER PLAY
To ask good questions, it helps to first think about the subject as much as possible.

Using the skills and knowledge you listed, work with your partner to think of 5 questions you would ask someone who applied to you for that job. Write your questions below.

_____

_____

_____

_____

_____

_____

_____

_____

Frank Schaffer Publications

SHOW, DON'T TELL

Have you ever seen a set of instructions that used only pictures, and not words, to communicate the message? Many road signs use pictures and symbols to communicate messages such as "No left turn" and "Turn right to get to the airport." Picture instructions can also be used for more complicated tasks, such as building a model or hooking up a stereo system.

Your **POWERTHINKING** challenge is to research and design a step-by-step instructional poster for a complicated task, using only pictures. Here are some possible subjects for your poster.

> How to Ride a Bicycle
> How to Make a Garden Salad
> How to Make a Pitcher of Lemonade
> How to Plant a Tree

POWER PLAY

After you have drawn your pictures, try to follow your directions. Write down what happened. Did you forget a step? Did you include a step that wasn't necessary? Compare your results with others in your class.

Name(s)_____

ARE SALES UP OR DOWN?

You are the president of Iceberg Cereal Company. Your bookkeeper left suddenly for a vacation in Jamaica. The records are a mess.
You find notes on scraps of paper in a shoe box in the bottom drawer.
Organize the notes to complete the chart on the bottom
of the page.

POWER PLAY
Sometimes you can solve a puzzle even if some of the pieces seem to be missing.

Feel free to work with a partner and use a calculator for this activity.

A couple of things you need to know:
    Profits = Sales — expenses.
    Each box of Iceberg Cereal sells for $3.28.

	Number of boxes sold	Dollar amount of sales	Business expenses	Profits
May	16,000			
June			$2,842.16	
July		$69,208.00		

ALLIGATOR REPELLENT

You've studied math in school. You know the basics. So how does math apply to real life?

One way your math skills can help is by saving you and your family money when you go shopping. Your **POWERTHINKING** skills can help too.

Here's the problem: Iceberg cereal comes in two sizes.
The 36-ounce size costs $4.78. The 24-ounce size costs $3.60.
Which is the better buy?

How do you figure this problem out?_____

_____

What if you had to make a choice between eight 12-ounce cans of alligator repellent that total $5.28 and seven 16-ounce cans for a total of $5.50?

Work with a partner to break this problem down into steps. Talk about each step of solving the problem. First list the steps.

Step 1: _____

_____

Step 2: _____

_____

Step 3: _____

_____

Step 4: _____

_____

Now go back and solve the problem. Which is the better buy — eight 12-ounce cans or seven 16-ounce cans? Use the back of this page if you need it.

POWER PLAY

With a partner, imagine something you'd like to buy at the store. But don't think of something that already exists, make something up. Each of you pick a size, price, and how many you'd like to buy.

Use the steps in the Alligator Repellent problem to figure out whose purchase would be the better buy.

NOT A RECTANGLE

Sometimes problems look difficult at first. Some people throw their hands up in the air and say, "I can't!" They give up before they even get started.

You already know how to find the area of a rectangle: multiply the length times the width. Using that knowledge, how would you find the area of this figure?

Shape A

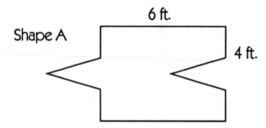

6 ft.

4 ft.

How can knowing how to find the area of a rectangle help you find the area of this funny looking shape? It's not a rectangle. Anyone can see that at a glance. Or is it?

Imagine a rectangle that has had the center "pushed over" a little. Would it look like Shape A? Mentally "push" the jagged part back into place. Now what shape is it? What's the area of the shape?

How about the next two? Find the area of Shapes B and C.

Shape B

Shape C

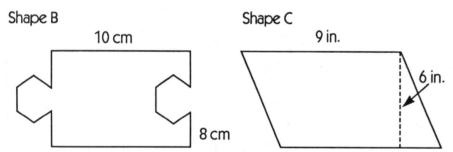

10 cm

8 cm

9 in.

6 in.

Work with a partner. Talk about how to solve each problem.

Now answer these questions.

What is the area of shape A? _____

What is the area of shape B? _____

What is the area of shape C? _____

POWER PLAY
Problems that seem difficult at first can sometimes be made simple by applying what you already know. Looking at a problem from a different angle can help. Be persistent!

NOT A MATH TEST

How do you feel about taking a math test? What if the test consisted entirely of word problems? Don't groan. Don't worry either. This isn't a math test, and the only word problem is the one **you** will be writing.

The hardest part of a word problem is figuring out how to set up the steps to solve it.

Work with a partner to think of a word problem that could be used on a test for your class. Once you've written the problem, write out each step needed to solve it. Talk through the questions and steps with your partner before writing them down.

State the problem here:

_____

_____

_____

_____

_____

POWER PLAY

How can making up a word problem of your own help you understand the steps of solving other similar problems?

List the steps, in order, needed to solve your problem. Use the back of the page if you need more room.

1. _____

_____

2. _____

_____

3. _____

_____

4. _____

_____

The answer to our problem is:_____

_____

MAGIC SQUARE

If you were asked to arrange the numbers 1, 2, 3, 4, and 5 in the square below so that the sum of each row equals 15, that would be simple. 1 + 2 + 3 + 4 + 5 = 15.

But, you're not going to get off that easily! To really get you to **POWERTHINK**, each column must also add up to 15 and the two diagonals must must also add up to 15.

Work with a partner to arrange the numbers so that each row across adds up to 15, each column down adds up to 15 and both diagonals equal 15.

Be sure to use a pencil so you can erase. Talk with your partner about where to place the numbers as you work.

Hint: The same number cannot appear more than once in the same row, column or diagonal.

POWER PLAY

Write a set of step-by-step instructions that would guide someone through solving a magic square problem with a "magic" sum of 16. There are several right answers to this number square. After you have found one, see if you can find others.

15

15

15

15

15

15

15 15 15 15 15

15

INVENT IT!

An inventor rarely invents something for no reason at all. Usually, inventions are born out of the need to combine a **process** with an **object** in a new **environment**. How strong are your powers of invention? Figure out a way to randomly pick a number between 111 and 999. You could pull numbers out of a hat or ask a friend to "pick a number."

Use your random number to fill in the blanks in the sentence below. Use the first digit for the number to fill in the blank numbered "1", the second digit to fill in the blank numbered "2", and the third digit to fill in the blank numbered "3". Then, read the sentence and do what it says!

Column A Process What does it do?	Column B Object What does it do it to?	Column C Environment Where does it happen?
1. transport	1. a hippopotamus	1. on the moon
2. wash	2. a jackhammer	2. in outer space
3. paint	3. a computer	3. in a jungle
4. chill	4. a motorcycle	4. in an art museum
5. throw	5. a bouquet of flowers	5. at the top of a skyscraper
6. hide	6. a beehive	6. in your room at home
7. measure	7. a washing machine	7. in a library
8. dry off	8. a cookie	8. in a fire station
9. pulverize	9. a fried egg	9. in a desert

Invent a machine that will:

_____ , _____ _____
      1   2   3

POWER PLAY

Draw a picture of your invention and write a few sentences explaining how it works.

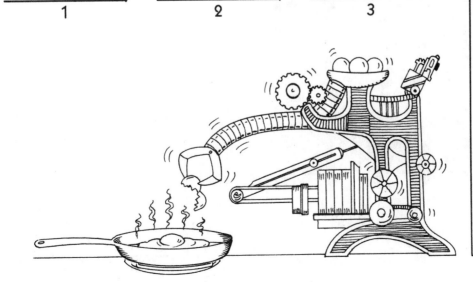

REDUCE, REUSE, RECYCLE

Today the three R's are Reduce, Reuse and Recycle. They are ways you can help cut down on the ever-growing trash problem. To **reduce** means to use less: less energy, less packaging, less food. To **reuse** an item means to find other uses for it instead of throwing it away. A **recycling** plant takes used or waste materials and makes them into new materials.

Select one of the items listed below. Work in a small group to **POWERTHINK** about ways to reduce, reuse, or recycle each of the objects. Ask one person to write down all ideas. Give all members of the group a chance to express their ideas.

Newspapers
    Plastic bottles
        Dead batteries
            Empty shoe boxes
                Glass jars
                    Plastic jugs
                        Egg cartons
                          Plastic bags
                            Used clothing
                              Old books
                                Old cars

POWER PLAY

With a partner, pick one of the ideas your group came up with and make a mobile.

LIMA BEANS ARE GREEN

When you read or listen to someone speak, you'll hear **facts** and **opinions**. A fact is a statement that can be proved. Facts can be verified through other sources.

An opinion is a belief that cannot be proven true or false. An opinion is what someone believes or thinks is true.

> Lima beans taste better than corn on the cob.
> Lima beans are green.

When you look at the two sentences above, it's easy to tell which is fact and which is opinion. But it's not always so obvious.

An opinion can be based on facts. Scientists often start with what they know and then form theories about what they don't know.
A theory may be an assumption, a prediction or a guess based on the available facts.

Once a theory can be proven it becomes a fact.

What are some sources you could use to decide if a statement is a fact or an opinion?

Work with a partner. Write a sentence. Ask your partner to give reasons why he or she thinks the sentence is a fact or an opinion. Take turns writing sentences and talking about them.

POWER PLAY

Which are better, facts or opinions? The two are different, but one is not necessarily better. However, as a ***POWERTHINKER*** *you want to be able to distinguish between the two.*

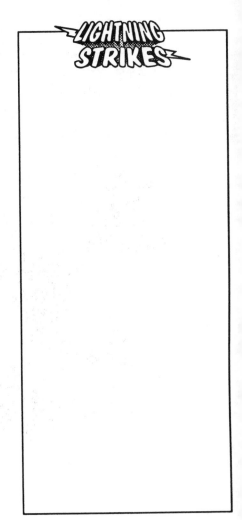

Sentence	Fact or Opinion?	Why?

Name(s)_____

PEREGRINE FALCONS ARE ENDANGERED

Work with a partner. Read each sentence about peregrine falcons. Do some **POWERTHINKING** and talk about whether the sentence is fact or opinion. Put an **O** in the space after the sentence if it is an opinion. Put an **F** if it is a fact that could be verified as true or false.

1. Falcons are beautiful birds.   _____

2. They make their nests high up on the sides of cliffs
   or mountains.   _____

3. Watching the courtship displays of the male peregrine
   is a thrilling experience.   _____

4. The males perform loops and dives of over
   2,000 feet, reaching speeds of up to 200 miles
   per hour.   _____

5. Once found in all parts of the world except
   Antarctica, peregrine falcons are an endangered
   species today.   _____

6. The use of DDT as a pesticide has caused
   their near-extinction.   _____

7. Falcons eat smaller birds that feed on grain
   sprayed with DDT.   _____

8. DDT causes falcons to lay eggs with shells so thin
   they break when the females sit on them.   _____

9. It must be very sad for the poor mother falcons. _____

10. Even though the use of DDT has been banned in
    the U.S., falcons in this country are still in danger. _____

11. They migrate to countries that still use DDT and
    feed on migratory birds that have eaten grain
    sprayed with DDT.   _____

12. Countries that use DDT don't care about falcons. _____

POWER PLAY
*When you read, why is it important to know
if the statements are facts or opinions?*

Frank Schaffer Publications

FS112115 POWERTHINK

YOU'RE THE INVENTOR

You've read about and studied many famous inventors. One thing many of them have in common is they ask the question, WHAT IF? and then try to find the answer. Asking the "WHAT IF?" question is something **POWERTHINKERS** are very good at.

Before you read any further, you and your partner should select a number between 111 and 999. Write the number here. _____

Now look at the three columns below. Find the word or phrase from each column to match the number you selected. If your number was 376, your words would be WOOD, A PIE PAN, CRAYONS.

What could you invent using these three objects in some way? Perhaps you could color the wood and build a bird feeder using the pie pan to hold the bird food?

POWER PLAY

With your partner, draw a picture or diagram of your invention. Exchange pictures with another group. Look at the picture that was given to you. What do you think that invention is? What does it do?

Column A	Column B	Column C
1. tomato	book	shoes
2. tape	clock	yarn
3. wood	beans	paper
4. long pole	bricks	tires
5. battery	straw	calendar
6. extension cord	a tree	crayons
7. pencil	a pie pan	deck of cards
8. ruler	5 yards of cotton	a wheel
9. dictionary	gears	scraps of leather

Write your three words: _____, _____, _____

What can you invent using those three objects?

Describe your invention. What would it do? How would it work? What would it look like? Why do we need it?

_____

_____

_____

_____

_____

_____

MERCURY OLYMPICS

Although we cannot see it, hear it, smell it, taste it, or touch it, gravity surrounds you and prevents you from floating off into space.

Gravity affects how much you weigh, how much you can lift, how high you can jump, and how far you can throw a ball. Gravity changes from planet to planet, depending on the size of the planet. On giant Jupiter, where the gravity is three times as powerful as on Earth, you would weigh three times as much! You could lift only one-third as much, and jump only one-third as high.

The moon is much smaller than Earth. The gravity on the moon is only about one-sixth that of Earth. If you weighed 100 pounds on Earth, you would weigh about 17 pounds on the moon.

Imagine holding the Olympics on Mercury, a planet with one-third the gravity of Earth. Describe several events and how they would be different on Mercury.

Some Olympic events you could consider are wrestling, skiing, gymnastics, diving, basketball, high jump, pole vaulting, running, and swimming.

Event: _____

How would it be different?_____

_____

_____

What would the "Mercury record" be in this event?

_____

Event: _____

How would it be different?_____

_____

_____

What would the "Mercury record" be in this event?

_____

POWER PLAY
What new Olympic event could be held on Mercury that would be impossible to hold on Earth?

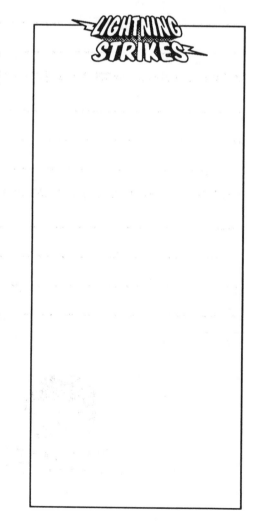

A TERRIFIC TOY

You and your partner have been hired to design a magazine ad for a new toy. The ad can appeal to either children or their parents. You may not use any words in the ad except the name of the toy, which you also have to invent.

The toy is a plastic box with switches, buttons, and knobs. It plays a song, flashes different lights, buzzes, whirs, beeps, purrs, ticks, barks, moos, and crackles.

By the way, the toy costs $399.95, so be convincing!

You can draw, color, paint, or cut out pictures from magazines and paste them in place to make your ad. Use another sheet of paper.

After you finish your ad, answer these questions:

Is your ad designed to appeal to children or parents?

_____

How would your ad be different if it appealed to the other group?

_____

_____

Looking at your ad, what message will people get?

_____

_____

_____

Why should someone buy this product?

_____

_____

_____

_____

POWER PLAY
The people who design ads know that colors and illustrations will appeal to different types of people. The idea is to sell the product by giving people a reason to want to buy it.

FS112115 POWERTHINK

Frank Schaffer Publications

SHOW ME

You have probably studied or read about the effects of water pollution on fish and other types of wildlife. In many places, water is unsafe to drink. Beaches are closed to swimmers.

Sometimes, simply showing the consequences of water pollution is more convincing than talking about it. Design a poster that makes a statement about the effects of water pollution without using any words.

Use this sheet for your poster.

What message do you want people to get when they look at your poster?

_____

_____

_____

POWER PLAY
Why can a drawing sometimes be more effective than words?

LIGHTNING STRIKES

Name(s)_____

YOUR FAMILY FLAG

The U.S. flag has 50 stars, one for each state. The 13 red and white stripes stand for the 13 original colonies. Different countries use different colors, symbols, and arrangements that stand for things that are important to that country.

What would your family flag look like? If you lived on a farm, your flag might include a barn. A boat or a lake could be on the flag of a family that liked water sports.

Before you start designing your family flag, think about and answer these questions.

What colors will you use? _____

Why did you select those colors? _____

_____

Will you use geometric shapes like stars, triangles, squares, circles, stripes or octagons? Explain why you plan to use each shape.

_____

_____

_____

_____

_____

What other shapes or symbols will you use?_____

_____

What do the shapes or symbols stand for?_____

_____

_____

How will your flag be shaped? _____

Why did you select that shape? _____

_____

_____

Design your family flag using crayons, paints, markers, strips of colored paper, or whatever media is available. Use the back of this page or a different sheet of paper.

POWER PLAY

You see symbols in art, literature, and even television. What those symbols stand for is important.

With a partner, page through a magazine or watch a television program. Make a list of symbols you see. Keep going until you have listed 50 symbols. What are the most common shapes and images? Think up a way to classify the symbols. For example, you could classify them by design: Abstract or Realistic. Or by function: Advertising (logos and trademarks), Cartographical (map symbols), or Mathematical.

"Turn right at the corner where they cut down the apple tree, go past the empty lot where the blue car is usually parked, and then to the house that used to be white. Turn left where Mr. Lorenzo used to live. You can't miss it."

Would those directions help you find your way? Can you give better directions? Work with a partner who has not seen the pictures on this page.

The numbers 1 to 15 mark the rows. The letters A to O mark the columns. Choose one of the pictures. Give a copy of the next page, "Did You Follow That?", to a partner. By giving coordinates on the grid, tell your partner which squares to fill in to match the picture you chose. Don't watch while your partner draws.

When you finish, compare your partner's drawing to the one you selected. How close did you come?

POWER PLAY

Try this activity again using your own picture. Use the grid below.

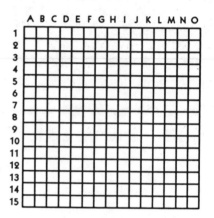

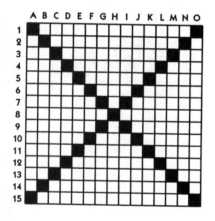

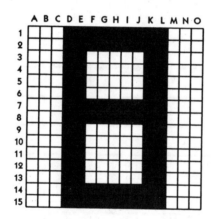

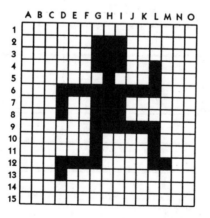

DID YOU FOLLOW THAT?

"Turn right at the corner where they cut down the apple tree, go past the empty lot where the blue car is usually parked, and then to the house that used to be white. Turn left where Mr. Lorenzo used to live. You can't miss it."

Would those directions help you find your way?

The numbers 1 to 15 mark the rows. The letters A to O mark the columns. Your partner will give coordinates for coloring specific squares to make a picture on the grid. Do not look at your partner's picture and don't let your partner see your drawing until you've finished.

When you finish, compare your drawing to the picture your partner selected. How close did you come?

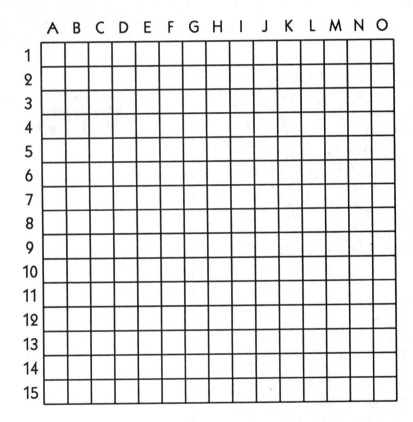

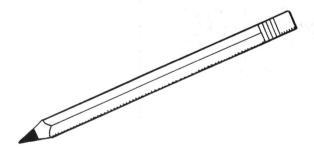

POWER PLAY

Why is it important to give clear, precise directions?

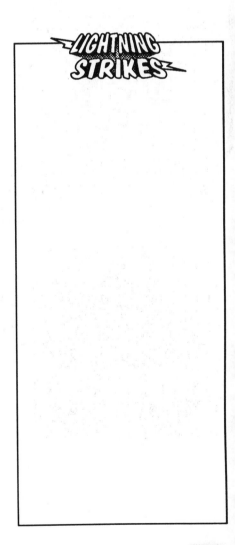

MAKE A MOBILE POINT

For this project, you will need a clothes hanger, some string, thread or fishing line, and some pictures or small objects.

Use the ideas your group came up with in the activity titled "Reduce, Reuse, Recycle" as a starting point for making a class mobile. Work with a partner or in small groups.

Find or make small, lightweight objects or drawings, or find pictures in a magazine appropriate to some of the ideas your group discussed.

Cut out your drawings or pictures and paste them on a piece of light cardboard. Punch a small hole in the cardboard and tie a string to the objects and pictures. Use string, thread, or fishing line to attach them to the hanger.

Display the mobile in your classroom or take it home and share it with your family.

POWER PLAY
Ideas can be communicated without words.

DECISIONS, DECISIONS, DECISIONS

To **decide** means to make a choice between two or more options. You make many decisions every day from the time you wake up in the morning until you fall asleep at night.

Should I get up today?
What should I have for breakfast?
What book should I read?
Should I study for the math test or watch a movie?

POWERTHINKING can help you make decisions you feel good about. The secret is to take the decision one step at a time. Work with a partner and begin at the beginning.

STEP 1: State the question as simply as possible.

Two of your friends, Terry and Kym, are each having a party next Saturday and both of them want you to come. You can only go to one party.

The question is: _____

_____

Now that you know the question, what's next?

STEP 2: List the goals you want to achieve.

For the question about which party to go to, your goals could be:

1. Have fun.

2. Do not hurt Terry's feelings.

3. Do not hurt Kym's feeling.

Add at least three more goals.

4. _____

5. _____

6. _____

POWER PLAY

Before you can make a decision, you need to be straight on what the question is, then decide what you want to accomplish.

WHAT ARE YOUR OPTIONS?

You've gone a long way toward making your decision. You've used **POWERTHINKING** to figure out exactly what the question is, and the goals you want to reach with your decision. Now the task is to examine your **options**. Options are choices you can make.

STEP 3: List your options.

1. Go to Terry's party.

2. Go to Kym's party.

3. Don't go to either party.

What other options are there? Discuss possibilities with your partner. List at least three more options.

4. _____
   _____

5. _____
   _____

6. _____
   _____

POWER PLAY

When you have to make a decision, you'll want as many options as possible. The options aren't always obvious. Sometimes it takes some hard thinking to come up with lots of good ideas.

GETTING CLOSER

Well, you've **POWERTHOUGHT** yourself halfway through this sticky problem! You've identified the question, stated your goals and listed your options. Now it's time to take the next step.

STEP 4: List the pros and cons for each option.

Look at each of the options. List reasons for (pros) and against (cons) each one. Most options will have both pros and cons.

Option 1: Go to Terry's party

Pros	Cons
Terry has better food	*Kym would feel hurt*
Terry would be happy	*Terry doesn't play good music*
Best friends will be at Terry's	*Won't know many people there*

Option 2: Go to Kym's party

Pros   Cons

_____   _____

_____   _____

_____   _____

Option 3: Don't go to either party. Have your own party.

Pros   Cons

_____   _____

_____   _____

_____   _____

Option 4: _____

Pros   Cons

_____   _____

_____   _____

_____   _____

Option 5: _____

Pros   Cons

_____   _____

_____   _____

_____   _____

LIGHTNING STRIKES

 Frank Schaffer Publications

FINALLY...

Deciding which party to attend has been difficult, but you're almost finished. Just a little more **POWERTHINKING** and you'll have a decision you can feel good about.

Remember the goals you wrote? Look back at them. Then go on to...

STEP 5: Compare options.

Compare each option with your list of goals. Look closely at the pros and cons for each option.

What do you think your two best options are?

_____

_____

Why did you select these options?

_____

_____

Now it's time to...

STEP 6: Make a decision.

What did you decide to do?

_____

REVIEW: The six **POWERTHINKING** steps for making a decision are:

1. State the question.
2. List your goals.
3. List your options.
4. List pros and cons for each option.
5. Compare options.
6. Make a decision.

POWER PLAY

You need to make decisions every day. These six steps can help make the process easier.

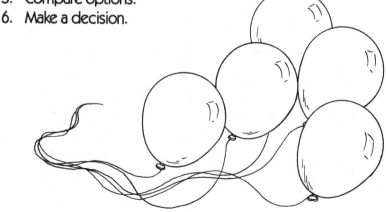

WHAT, ME WORRY?

It's a gorgeous day today; warm and sunny.

Maybe, but today is too beautiful not to enjoy it.

I hear it's supposed to rain hard tomorrow.

I can't help worrying about the rain tomorrow.

Which person are you most like, Sally or Jay?

Some people never worry about anything. Others worry constantly. The trick is to be somewhere in between: to worry about important things without letting them take over your life, and to ignore the unimportant things.

What if the world is invaded by giant beetles from Venus?
What if I don't pass my science test?
What if the sun never rises again?
What should I wear to Saturday's party?
What would I do if I suddenly broke out in green spots?

You can't do much about the giant beetles, the sun, or green spots, even if they do happen. And chances are, they probably won't.

You could plan study time to pass your science test and look through your closet to see what you'll wear to the party.

Sometimes it helps to classify worries into ones you can do something about and the ones you can't.

List some worries you can't do anything about.

_____

_____

List a few things you worry about that you know you can handle with a little **POWERTHINKING**.

_____

_____

Of the ones you know you can handle, what can you do about them?

_____

_____

That little worry in the back of your mind may be trying to tell you something. Take a look at it. Is it important? If not, put it in your pocket and forget about it.

POWER PLAY
People waste time and energy by worrying about things they can't do anything about.

GETTING A HANDLE ON WORRIES

When something worries you, one way to **POWERTHINK** about it is to visualize it as an object. Is it small enough to hold in your hand? Is it large enough to smother an elephant? Does it fill the whole room?

Now ask yourself, what can I do about it? If you're sure the answer is "absolutely nothing," ask yourself how likely it is to happen.

If the chances are pretty low that it could happen, put that worry on the back shelf of your closet and shut the door. Forget about it for now. It will always be there if you need it.

What if you have a really big worry about something that is likely to happen — for example, if you needed an operation or were moving to a new city?

Try going through the steps you learned for decision making. If that doesn't work, what other options do you have?

Talking to someone about your worries can help you see them in a new light.

Name some people you could talk to about a personal or family situation that is worrying you.

_____

_____

What if you were worried about a lump growing on your arm?

_____

_____

What if you were having big problems in school? Who could you talk to?

_____

_____

POWER PLAY
Don't forget to enjoy the good times. Put worries in their proper place. If you need help, ask for it.

SEEING THE OTHER SIDE

People have different tastes, opinions, and points of view (ways of looking at something). There are dozens of reasons for these differences. Work with a partner. Do some **POWERTHINKING** and list several reasons why people see the world differently.

Thinking about why people might disagree with you should help you be open-minded. Always try to listen to other points of view.

Do you agree with this statement?

> Parents have the right to control the amount of time and type of programs children watch on television. This includes home videos and movies.

Practice seeing both points of view. List at least five reasons or ideas that support each side of this issue.

Parents have the right to control the amount of time and type of programs that children watch.

_____

_____

_____

_____

Parents should not control the amount of time and type of programs that children watch.

_____

_____

_____

_____

_____

POWER PLAY
Write about a time when someone failed to see things from your point of view. How did it make you feel? Why is it important to look at another's point of view?

MAYBE THERE'S ANOTHER WAY

Josh has taken the same route to school since he was in kindergarten. He turns right on Maple Avenue, goes two blocks, and turns left on South Street. Last night a wind storm knocked down trees and power lines on Maple Avenue. Today, the street is blocked off and no one is allowed through. Josh takes a look, decides he can't get to school today, and goes home.

"Well, that's not too bright," you might say. "Why doesn't he simply take another route?"

That's a good idea. Why didn't Josh think of that?

Sometimes people get so set in their ways — so used to doing something or looking at something in only one way — that they can't see any other possibilities.

Work with a partner. Talk about what could be done in each situation listed below. How many alternatives can you think of?

You lost your house key. The door is locked. No one else will be home for at least two hours. What can you do?

_____

_____

_____

Your dog ate your homework (really). You have one hour before it's due. Your friends are waiting to play baseball. What could you do?

_____

_____

_____

You promised to water the neighbor's plants while she was on vacation. You forgot. All the plants died. The neighbor will be home tomorrow. Now what?

_____

_____

_____

POWER PLAY

You forgot your history text and you have an open book test today. With your partner list as many possible solutions to the problem as you can.

USING THE TOOLS

A carpenter wouldn't begin a house without getting all the necessary tools and learning how to use them.

You've been learning many **POWERTHINKING** skills. They are like a carpenter's tools. They can help you solve many kinds of problems.

Imagine you will be giving a speech in front of the entire student body at the next assembly. You could use decision-making skills to decide on the topic of your speech.

List other **POWERTHINKING** skills you could use and how they could help you prepare and deliver your speech.

POWER PLAY
POWERTHINKING *skills you learn in one area can often help you in other areas.*

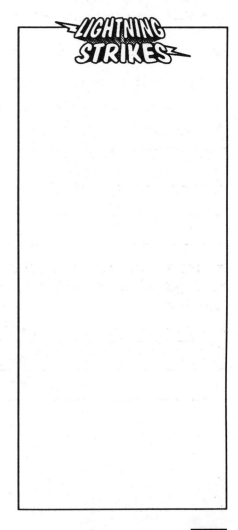

ENCOURAGING POWERTHINKING

One of the additional benefits of teaching critical thinking and problem solving in your classroom is that it is an excellent forum for positive reinforcement. Try some of these on for size!

That's an excellent question.

Perhaps that idea would work. Let's try it.

That's a creative way of looking at it.

Not many people would have come up with such an unusual idea.

Terrific idea!

Very interesting thought! Maybe it would work.

I never thought of it that way. Good idea!

That could be just the ticket!

That suggestion makes a lot of sense.

That idea is pretty fantastic.

What a wonderful thought!

That suggestion is quite unique.

That shows you're really thinking.

Let's consider Joe's idea.

Very imaginative!

Splendid!

What a marvelous plan!

Let's consider Sue's recommendation.

Very creative!

Let's give Kim a round of applause for that suggestion.

Very inventive!

Let's follow Tim's line of thinking and see where it goes.

Now why didn't I think of that? Good job.

How did you ever think of such a good idea?

Congratulations on coming up with that solution.

You're very observant!

Your good ideas are popping like popcorn.

That could be just the answer we need.

All right!

That idea shows you're really thinking.

You're quite a **POWERTHINKER.**

Your question shows you put a lot of thought into the problem.

You're really thinking today!

Good going!

That's a pretty awesome idea!

Brilliant idea!

You're very creative.

Great plan!

I knew you could figure out an answer for yourself.

You handled that tough problem very well.

Wow! I'm impressed.

You made a wise decision.

You handled that problem well.

Brilliant!

Jill has the hang of it now.

What an interesting proposal!

This class is full of good ideas today.

See what you can accomplish!

Working together really works.

Well done!

I can't believe all the great ideas you've had today.

Nice job!

Keep up the good work.

That is so outrageous it's contagious!

Frank Schaffer Publications
FS112115 POWERTHINK

BIBLIOGRAPHY

For Teachers:

Heiman, Marcia and Slomianko, Joshua. Critical Thinking Skills.
  Washington, DC: National Education Association, 1986.
Moore, Brooke Noel and Parker, Richard. Critical Thinking.
  Mountain View, CA: Mayfield Publishing Company, 1986.
Van Oech, Roger. A Kick in the Seat of the Pants.
  New York: Harper & Row, 1986.
Van Oech, Roger. A Whack on the Side of the Head.
  New York: Warner Books, 1990.
Cobb, Vicki. How to REALLY Fool Yourself: Illusions for All Your Senses.
  Philadelphia, PA: J.B. Lippincott, 1981.
Costa, Arthur A. Developing Minds: A Resource Book for Teaching Thinking, Volumes I and II.
  Washington, DC: Association for Supervision and Curriculum Development, 1991.
Curriculum Update. Washington, DC: Association for Supervision and Curriculum Development. June, 1993.

For Students:

Bendick, Jeanne. Observation.
  New York: Franklin Watts, Inc., 1972.
Berry, Joy. Every Kid's Guide to Handling Feelings.
  Chicago: Children's Press, 1986.
Berry, Joy. Every Kid's Guide to Thinking and Learning.
  Chicago: Children's Press, 1987.
Berry, Marilyn. Help is on the Way For: Thinking Skills.
  Chicago: Children's Press, 1986.
Bernards, Neal. Advertising: Distinguishing Between Fact and Opinion.
  San Diego: Greenhaven Press, Inc., 1963.
Burns, Marilyn. The Book of Think (Or How to Solve a Problem Twice Your Size).
  Boston: Little, Brown and Company, 1976.
Cobb, Vicki. How to REALLY Fool Yourself: Illusions for All Your Senses.
  New York: J.B. Lippincott, 1981.
Gould, Laurence J. and William G. Martin. Think About It: Experiments in Psychology.
  Englewood Cliffs, NJ: Prentice-Hall, Inc.,1968.
Simon, Seymor. The Optical Illusion Book.
  New York: Four Winds Press, 1976.
Tchudi, Stephen. The Young Learner's Handbook.
  New York: Charles Scribner's Sons, 1987.

page 16 — Chirp, Chirp, Boom, Creak.
Hint: The noises may not all be coming from one source. There could be one reason for the chirp, chirp, another for the crash and another for the boom. The sounds may not be related.

page 18 — Classification Puzzle.
1. vowels/non-vowels
2. letters with only straight lines/letters with curved and straight lines
3. letters that are not Roman numerals/letters that are Roman numerals

page 19 — Dr. Livingstone, I Presume.
Numbers 3, 4, and 5 are logical inferences.

page 26 — Distress Signals.
a. cannot proceed   b. safe to land   c. yes   d. going this way   e. need food and water   f. no

page 36 — Are Sales Up or Down?

	Number of boxes sold	Dollar amount of sales	Business expenses	Profits
May	16,000	$52,480	$13,120.00	$39,360.00
June	19,200	$62,976	$2,842.16	$60,133.84
July	21,100	$69,208	$2,482.02	$66,725.98

page 37 — Alligator Repellent.
1. Multiply 8 by 12 to find out how many total ounces if you buy eight 12-ounce cans (96).
2. Divide the cost (5.28) by the number of ounces (96) to find the cost per ounce (5.5 cents per ounce).
3. Multiply 7 by 16 to find out how many total ounces if you buy seven 16-ounce cans (112).
4. Divide the cost (5.50) by the number of ounces (112) to find the cost per ounce (4.9 cents per ounce).
5. The seven 16-ounce cans are the better buy.

page 38 — Not a Rectangle.
Shape A = 24 square feet, Shape B = 80 cm^2, Shape C = 54 square inches.

page 40 — Magic Square.
There are several combinations that will work. Here are three of them:

```
1 4 5 3 2     4 3 1 2 5     1 5 2 3 4
5 2 4 1 3     3 5 2 4 1     4 2 1 5 3
2 1 3 5 4     2 1 3 5 4     5 4 3 2 1
3 5 2 4 1     5 2 4 1 3     3 1 5 4 2
4 3 1 2 5     1 4 5 3 2     2 3 4 1 5
```

page 44 — Peregrine Falcons Are Endangered.
1. O, 2. F, 3. O, 4. F, 5. F, 6. F, 7. F, 8. F, 9. O, 10. F, 11. F, 12. O.